Wakefield Press

drums & bonnets

Miriel Lenore was born in Boort, Victoria, and was educated there and in Bendigo and Melbourne. She worked as a plant breeder, student counsellor, teacher and writer and editor of Fijian church publications. After twenty-two years in Fiji, and a brief period in Sydney, she moved to Adelaide where she still lives.

Miriel began writing poetry in 1984 during a Women's Studies course. Her recent interests include Rock Art, Botanic Gardens and the exploration of the lives of several women in her family's history. *drums & bonnets* presents the first of these and Wakefield Press will bring out a second book in 2004.

T0363964

drums & bonnets

miriel lenore

Wakefield
Press

Wakefield Press
1 The Parade West
Kent Town
South Australia 5067
www.wakefieldpress.com.au

First published 2003

Cover painting by Katherine Stafford
Cover designed by Lahn Stafford Design
Text designed and typeset by Clinton Ellicott
Printed and bound by Hyde Park Press

National Library of Australia
Cataloguing-in-publication entry

Lenore, Miriel.
Drums & bonnets.

ISBN 1 86254 628 2.

I. Title.

A821.3

Wakefield Press thanks Fox Creek Wines
and Arts South Australia for their support.

Publication of this book was assisted by the
Commonwealth Government through the
Australia Council, its arts funding and advisory body.

for

David, Caroline & Libby

Looking backwards, we could only be searching for ourselves.

Gustaf Sobin

Contents

the land of Macha

the emigrants
after the painting by James Wilson, 1852, Belfast

the crowded ship has pulled out into the stream

on the quay a woman sobs
a man lifts his hat on a stick to signal
                    over the widening gulf
another woman turns her back to the ship
                    hides with her hand her eyes
a little boy in his best suit is troubled by all this weeping
two Arabian merchants watch in silence
boys fish from the jetty
cool as the man ploughing
            while a god falls from the sky

the passengers wave and laugh –
            their lives widen with the gap

to the right of the jetty the land is bare

encounter

you look lost
the young man could be a student
showing me the way to the Lagan
     my first afternoon in Belfast
he's a photographer doing a book
        on the Travellers
most marginalised people in Ireland
I've come to see my great-grandmother's
country of Portadown and Tandragee

hey – he was born in Tandragee
his mother was a Quinn from there
but his father used mixed gangs at work
     there were death threats to his wife
so the family moved to England

he came back – he loves it here
     you're fine if when you speak
     you say nothing
        modish advice for a poet

at the river we say goodbye as old friends
     this Ulster journey will be good

capital city

a wee stamp for my letter
a wee lift to the second floor
a wee ticket for the bus where
smiling passengers offer a seat
give detailed directions

in Belfast's Botanic Gardens
six groups play soccer around the sign
No Ball Games

driver no 71:
we're Olympic champions at throwing
both sections: stones & bombs
best in the world at car burning too

laughing police in riot gear joke with
pert young girls
in the back of an armoured car

the peace wall

that wall to keep neighbour from neighbour
now has a softening ribbon of shrubs

once again the gates are locked
and the Army post on top of the hospital
reached only by helicopter keeps constant watch

on each side groups have been refurbishing
their murals for the marching season:
the Falls Road has a Madonna and child
                     a portrait of Bobby Sands
the flags of the Republic and old Ulster – and slogans:
        Equality is new and strong
        Our revenge will be the laughter of our children
        England all out for 32

over the wall in Shankill Road
the biggest mural shows four masked gunmen
flanking the motto *For God and Ulster*
beside Union Jacks Red Hands of Ulster
flags of the paramilitary
portraits of commandos
shorter messages:
        No Popery No Surrender
        Simply the Best
        Defiant till Death

the marching season

the band of fife and drum is coming closer
has already passed the bonfire
      where the Irish flag will burn

my heart beat rises to the rhythm
      as my blood runs cold
can heart and head be so much out of step?

      at the top of Sandy Row
the band in their smart blue uniforms
follow an Orange flag and a Union Jack
as sombre-suited men march in bowler hats
      and bright Orange sashes

women in Sunday dresses
      wait at the Lodge hall
they've been to church

the band breaks into
      What a friend we have in Jesus
      as I break into tears
for this divided country
      and for another I lived in –

Fijian Christians sang this hymn
      Jisu sa Wekada dina
as they held their government captive
      afraid of the Indians' power

poor Jesus
      so often called on for wars
no wonder he wept
as he saw people drowning
and all the while, he knew there was no river.

County Armagh
the heights of Macha

this county honours that powerful pregnant
queen who raced the swift horses of Conor
       gave birth to twins while dying
her name to the fort Emain Macha

from here Deidre eloped with the lover she heard
       singing on the ramparts
around here Queen Medb fought the Ulstermen
       for the Brown Bull of Cooley

here Miss Millicent Sparrow built dispensaries
       libraries and churches for her tenants
believing that much is required of those
       to whom much is given

Elizabeth Grimason survived here
       for eighty-seven years
paid threepence for winding twenty spools of linen

here her daughter Lizzie at seventeen
       set off alone to the world's end
knowing she wouldn't see home again

the Bannview Squash Club

are you sure it won't be too Country Club?
the Belfast assistant reassures me –
Portadown is not a tourist town

she is right: the grey cement block
has no visible name
no view of the River Bann
no obvious entrance
and seems totally deserted

a truck roars up and the driver
in paint-spattered overalls leaps
with the heartiest *hullo hullo welcome*
to give me an exuberant kiss

come in
we go upstairs and downstairs
past dumbells ladders and planks
towards a cup of tea:
                    he is mine host

my room has a view of grey wall
but I am moved to a windowless cell
when journalists appear for the march

at breakfast the landlord ignores me
to talk of the night's Troubles with them

Mary Street

first morning in my ancestors' town
excited hopeful
                            alien
somewhat bemused
where are the orchards?
                            the green fields?

my great-great-grandmother
that earlier Elizabeth Grimason
wrote at least one letter from Mary Street

the landlord is vague: *near West street*
past the church
                down by the railway
                            but it might have gone

it has

I picture Elizabeth here
growing old amongst her husband's relatives
walking to church and for mail
                writing to children overseas of Aunt Molly
Aunt Anna Uncle Will and sons returning from India

she worked until at eighty-three *My leg Brok*
and she spent *these last 4 years in My bed*

open space has replaced her tiny cottage –
a tangle of roadways and roundabouts
leads off the motorway
                            linking Belfast to Armagh
wide enough for tanks

Sid

what man would build
on one of the loveliest sites in town
        a pimple-on-a-pumpkin cabin?

a broad drive sweeps through noble gates
to curve up to the little white house
                above the river
high walls contain old glasshouses
                greeneries and sheds
an orchid appears through broken glass

Sid is fading fast a neighbour says
so I hurry lest I miss the nearest relative I've found.
                too frail to visit his plants
stiffened hips and damaged lungs keep him
            coughing inside the cabin

he was a tailor like his father and grandfather
grew prolific tomatoes under glass
mushrooms in his sheds
now he waits for his last outing

this man shares my family name
but knows nothing of Lizzie
you can't trace the family far he says
            the name varies too much
(yes – Lizzie and her mother spell it differently)

his branch were Army tailors in India
I see links – Lizzie's brothers also served there
and the same first names recur

I'm excited – want to explore these possible kin
Sid is not interested – breathing is his concern

Portadown
port of the fortress

I have long felt that Portadown is the Alabama of this island
                                                    Gerry Adams

a town where people might keep greyhounds or pigeons
a town with grey streets
even the red white & blue bunting has a dismal air
the ceremonial arches with their cannon crowns and bibles
recalling past battles against their countrymen
                    are props from a dated musical

with curfews and closures this is not the best time for research:
army helicopters trap the town under umbrellas of noise
become more deafening as they take off and land
four soldiers with guns at the ready peer
            from each armoured car patrolling the streets

when foot soldiers cover each other across High Street
I'm an extra in a B-grade movie hoping for no mistakes
part of me enjoys this heightened excitement
            pictures myself centre stage back home –
almost front line
            I have walked the Garvaghy Road
through the immense steel slabs that can shut in a moment etc

the waitress assures me I'll be safe if I'm in before dark
even as she recounts the troubles in Jervis Street

walking along the river I reach locked gates under the bridge
read the graffiti on the wall:
    Kill all Taigs

    this is not a movie

the Garvaghy Road

Nightly clashes have taken place between Portadown Orange Order supporters and security forces since Sunday's march down the nationalist Garvaghy Road was halted.

Sunday Life July 2 2000

women with plastic bags of groceries
talk of a sick neighbour
while helicopters rattle overhead

the Orange Order can't march down this public street
the past has filled the roadway
not the times before history
the times of stone axes & points & burial mounds
nor the times when pilgrims came to St Patrick's Well
not even when people paid taxes to the Pope –
                   those times lie quietly

the last four hundred years are still alive:
the McCann estates taken for the English
pillaged and burnt by furious McCanns
settlers thrown into the river and drowned
houses burnt rebuilt burnt rebuilt
then the Boyne and three hundred unjust years
to shape a town divided
              at the centre of the Murder Triangle

heavy freight for an ordinary street

Corcrain

all is quiet this morning in Corcrain
where my relatives once lived

I might not be safe here at night
in this week before the Drumcree march
when residents sing incendiary songs
fire guns burn bonfires of hate

if my great-grandmother had stayed
would she have stood with the haters?
would I?

our precarious selves

No 7 Carleton Street a plain
grey house flush with the path
in a line of similar dwellings
here Elizabeth came to receive mail
from her children on three continents

three windows stare across to the bowls
of purple petunias outside the Orange Lodge
where Union Jacks fly
we are also British says the sign

down the street a wall of graffiti
faces the school bus stop:
Simpson is fat
   Richard Day is gay
      Hall is a screw
         Lisa and Smithy
           Kay and Eddy
        Mr Daw is a queer assed faget

Bennett's Bar

in the shadow of St Mark's Church of Ireland
                    the bar blends into the street
keeps its old-fashioned air
retains the little snugs where you can drink
                    with friends in private

I have no friends here
even the bartender is offhand
                    bored by my questions

I take my glass to a corner
to find James Joyce on the wall above me:
        Oh Ireland, my first and only love
        Where Christ and Caesar are hand in glove

suddenly I'm not alone
                    and through the window see
the tired Union Jack hang on its pole
                    behind the locked gate of the church

Drumcree 2000

the posters are everywhere
in shop windows on postboxes and lightpoles
Drumcree 2000
Protestant Solidarity
Unite in our struggle against injustice.
'Unconquerable except by death.'

Bernadette Devlin says
if you answer Saint Anything
to the question *what school?*
you will never get the job

I read of a little boy wanting
to work in the Belfast shipyard
whose mother said *first*
you must change your name Patrick

marching to Drumcree

this town is used to Troubles:
thirty years my landlady says
my children know nothing else

cameras at the ready
my neighbours from the States
feel so lucky to be here today

the Orangeman in bronze looks down
from his pedestal next to the war memorial
where an angel tries to crown with laurels
                                    a falling soldier

old men with medals sashes swords
                    wear determined faces
No Surrender say their banners
but they cannot walk the Garvaghy Road

the younger men have worried foreheads
                        fewer medals no swords
you suspect their fathers insisted

the dozen women in the accordion bands
                        step out briskly
pleased to be part of the parade
playing Onward Christian Soldiers
                        Praise the Lord

the little boy who marches with his father
is learning a lesson difficult to unlearn
                    his sister carries a doll

the established church

three hundred years after they came
the English clung to the established
                Church of their betters
even when poor they knew they were
leagues above the Irish they displaced

when *the American War ruined the linen trade*
impoverishing her even more
Lizzie's mother still worried that the Whigs were
giving Popery so much liberty to keep in office
and Destroying a great Many good Landlords

and Elizabeth *did* have a good landlord
Miss Sparrow and her husband
now Duke and Duchess of Manchester
were Evangelical landlords fearful
                of God's judgement
should they misuse their privilege
so they built schools and dispensaries
devised loan funds and children's fetes
                and preserved
the true religion established among us

nine cases out of ten?

Sarah got married and got a very bad husband
            her mother's letters report on
her sister's marriage to
            an Artabracknagh man
keeps on wearing night and day

she had seven children and two dead
worked hard for the same people for years
moved often
(her husband does not stop long in one place)
and looked after her mother when she could
she is a verry good girl to me

the refrain is constant: *she got a bad husband*

her brother happily married in India
                    could philosophise:
nine cases out of ten unhappy marriages
            is caused by bad times and poverty
so we will drop the subject and hope
the next account we hear of them is better

her mother sent a lock of Sarah's hair to Lizzie
wished Sarah could also go
but she remained with the bad husband
who did not get better

Tandragee

*... its general appearance is prepossessing as seen from a distance,
ascending from a beautiful vale, through which the river Cusher
winds between its lofty and richly wooded banks at one extremity,
the demesne of Tanderagee crowning the hill at the other, forms a
strikingly picturesque feature in the landscape.*

S. Lewis 1837

my view is as beautiful as Lewis and Lizzie saw:
Tawnatelee Tawnatclec Tanrygee Tonregee
this place of many names and variations
            is still picturesque from Glebe Hill
the castle romantic in its demesne
                            next to the hilltop church

I leave the wealthy glebe lands
where Lizzie most certainly did not live
to pass *the most beautiful rectory in the county*
where a nearby quarry shakes walls
                            and makes plaster fall

I turn with the river around the flourmill
to climb the steep hill past the town stores –
six hairdressers four travel agents
                one baker and one grocer –
before I rest where church and castle meet

the approach from Armagh is less inviting
a new police fortress dominates
                           the crest of the hill
and armoured cars leave through steel slabbed gates
                  in its razor-wired fence
huge cement bollards could stop a tank or bomb

                           is it a comfort for some
that castle and church still overlook the police?

looking for Lizzie

opening the safe in the church office
the vicar turns
>   *what century did you want?*
I look at the 17th and 18th century books
>   *the 19th thanks*
the parson goes off trustingly to his service
leaving me with three hundred
>   years of church records
where Lizzie might be found

hours later frustration!
I know she was Church of Ireland
I know she was born here
I know her date of birth
>   and yet she isn't here
the many possible reasons for her absence
>   don't console me

I don't know where in the parish
her family stayed
was it in Ballysheilbeg
>   the little field tower
or Ballymore townland under the castle?
or along the Cusher river valley
>   towards Glen Clare?

only the bogs would have
prepared Lizzie for the quagmire
of early Ballarat

the quiet republican

after the service
I am invited to tea with an elderly congregation
          of eight women a man and the vicar
I learn of their Australian relatives
see postcards as proof of travels to France

when the tall worried man mentions politics
the air intensifies as all try to explain
their position their sense of betrayal

these Ulster Protestants want my understanding
know the world thinks them wrong
suspect I think them wrong
when they feel supremely right:
one of them said
          it sounds stupid but God is on our side
yet they are so troubled –
          I can offer no comfort

when I say goodbye to the vicar he whispers
I have to be quiet here
but I'm for union with the south
it's the only way

I understand his lowered voice
can barely tell my country town I vote Labor
not even whisper I'm lesbian

how much of Tandragee I wonder
did my great-grandmother bring to me?

the colonisers

the English learnt their colonising on us
the Irish say

there is a pattern:
first arrive with force and an extravagant
sense of right
drive out the natives to America
the other side of Shannon or Cooper's Creek

disparage those who remain:
their culture is boorish
their faith idolatrous
their habits lazy lying thieving and treacherous

ignore the ancient holy places:
the forts and ditches
the wells and standing stones
where this becomes impossible –
at Navan's great mound or Uluru –
make it a money spinner

name your sacred sites:
Church Street Mill Street Market Street
call your suburbs Brownstown or Redmondville

but the townlands have foiled you –
how to rename sixty-four in one parish?
Auglish Tullylinn Carrickbrack
            Corcreem and Lisnakee
resist as do Tjukala Yalata and Murrawidginie

Mr Tayto

after the majestic avenue of limes
             the Gothic turrets of faery lands or Dracula
the courtyard of brooding Tandragee castle
I walk under the sign of the swan to enter a modern passage lined
             with garish ads for potato crisps –
Rollers Whispers Bikers Wuster Sauce and more
I join a group of forty children as a potato-headed clown
welcomes us to Tayto Castle

after putting on protective gear – *Is ALL your hair covered?* –
we move through dungeons of potatoes
             rows of shiny machines with their aura of fat
are urged to check taste and texture at every stage
admire the machine which counts ten packs
             and the one whirring plastic around ten boxes
are loaded with crisps and information

the tours are booked three months ahead

this is not how I had pictured the castle
             on the site of O'Hanlons' old fort
rebuilt around the time of Lizzie's birth
I decide that her carpenter father
             worked here for Miss Sparrow
or rather the husband who gave her a coronet and gained an estate

after United States Cavalry were billeted here in World War II
and Colonel Edward M Fickett
                              trained them on Pig Point Flats
Mr Hutchinson bought the castle
sold the delicate chapel carvings to the parish church
a smoke-stained marble fireplace to the Montagu Arms
                              and created Mr Tayto

crack

in 1836 this town had thirty-six pubs
          I must select from four
The Paddock offers horsefloats and paintings of jockeys
          and is at the bottom of a very long hill
the Ballymore Arms is for sale
I choose the Montagu Arms since it promises
          olde worlde charm and 21st century technology

I may have done better with the horsy set
as every decibel from the Friday night band
          reverberates in my room over the bar
rolled towels along the doors don't help

at 1 a.m. I dress and go downstairs
          enter the bar ostentatiously to borrow a book
at 2.30 I go again to ask the closing time
shortly afterwards there is peace
          but I am too aware of the silence to sleep

the staff greet me kindly at breakfast
seem to forgive my failure to enjoy the crack
is my white hair again my saviour?

'crack' is the Anglo-Irish form of the craik: congenial conversation
or partying

the sham fight

long before Lizzie's birth
the village boys down the road at Scarva
fought the Battle of the Boyne each year
                    on the famous Thirteenth

no one got seriously hurt
when King James and his henchmen
                    were thrown in the river
for they were all good Protestant boys

these days fifty thousand people come
with plenty of food and drink
                    and bands
to celebrate a fight three hundred years ago

the battle is fought again at Scarva Field
                    where en route to the Boyne
King William camped under a chestnut tree

today no boys are thrown in the river and the kings
                    no longer ride on horseback
but still wear wigs and fancy coats
                    bring out their swords

the glorious moment is unchanged
when the Protestants crush the Catholics –
                the Orange Order and its Royal Blacks
resolve that no one in Ulster will ever forget

this year the Grand Master said people
                    came to enjoy themselves
they did not want to be offensive
                    or controversial

the Tandragee Man

one of Ireland's greatest kings
        three thousand years ago
Nuadha of the silver arm
lost his kingdom when his arm
        was lopped in battle
once wearing the silver replacement
        he soon won back his lands

found in a Tandragee yard
a stone Nuadha sits in Armagh cathedral
           holding his precious arm
his cavernous mouth like a weeping Pagliacci
        eyes wistful and suspicious:
from which direction his next adversary?

the land around him is blackened with blood –
this cathedral has been
        destroyed sixteen times
        restored sixteen times
      what more will this kingdom cost?

St Patrick by two

you say Armagh
and I see the hill
with the two tall spires or the square low tower
the faith of Patrick is with us still

John Hewitt

under its low tower on Drumsailloch
the Church of Ireland St Pat's
                           crowns the heights of Macha
where Daire finally gave Patrick
                  the land he wanted
this warm dark museum filled with
Celtic stones marble clergymen
                           and dusty regimental colours
has Brian Boru the last great Irish king
                  to guard it from the north

you are half way to heaven when
                  flanked by imperious prelates
you climb the steps of the Catholic St Pat's
enter this huge Victorian Gothic church
of light uncluttered space plain modern furniture
dried flowers for decoration
                           and no flags

only walking distance apart
                  the orange and green cathedrals
on their separate hills
            face each other across The Shambles

Maire Rua

when her husband was killed by Cromwell's men
Red Mary married one of them
to save the lands for her younger son

Jane Austen's matrons would understand
Jackie Onassis too
we do what we have to do at the crisis time

still it is a far cry from Maeve and Macha
and the wild queens
who fought for the bulls they wanted

and from those *old women on their hunkers*
old hags of the breasts
the Whore & the Witch   the Julia the Giddys

the Sheela na Gigs whose mouths gaped
in a fearsome grin
as they pulled their vaginas wide

to frighten away the evil
and delight those strong enough
to enjoy

art & life

if Western art's first picture of the Virgin and Child
is in the Book of Kells

the most erotic must surely be
in the Belfast Museum

the Carrickfergus Madonna half smiles
knowing how complex the mother-son bond

the little boy puts one hand around her neck
under her free-flowing hair

the other embraces her breast
her hands are spread wide fingers pressing his thigh

their mouths are a hairsbreadth from touching
they concentrate on ecstasy

Joseph is out of the picture out of his depth
a cause perhaps of all our wars

hands

St Patrick's hand is silver gilt
two bent fingers like the Buddha
blessing the world

on the O'Neills' red hand
(those traditional chiefs)
the fingers are spread

the open red hand of Ulster
has fingers close together
a policeman's warning

on the UFF posters
masked gunmen flank
a closed red fist

last chance

In the past eleven days 88 police and 6 soldiers have been injured
in 88 attacks on security forces, 236 have been arrested,
100 charged; 303 petrol bombs have been thrown, 1098 seized;
99 homes have been attacked and 86 other buildings;
417 vehicles have been damaged and 105 hijacked.

Belfast Telegraph 13/7/00

tomorrow the Records Office is closed
                              for the Belfast march
I must find Lizzie and her parents today
I hurry to sign in
          we close early today – the curfew
          when is early?
          2 pm – we must be home by 4
everything's against me
the index in use all the attendants busy

I race through the very few parishes
                    containing Grimasons
Ballymore? no Lizzie no Tom no Elizabeth
Drumcree? no
                    Kilmore? no Seagoe? no
last chance Mullaghbrack –
                    and the records have gone
Lizzie Tom and Elizabeth keep their mystery

at 1.30 we are pushed from the building
I walk to my guesthouse through frantic crowds
                              shopping for supplies
the air tense as before a Fiji hurricane

next morning I stroll to the corner for the big march:
the same Orange sashes and bowler hats
       same bands and hymns more Scots more pipes
same banners with King Billy upon his white horse
the Boy Jesus is there and founders of loyal Lodges
but marchers and crowds are more carefree
                        than at sombre Portadown

as the band plays Thine be the Glory
five marchers turn up our street
                   to piss in nearby front yards –
wombats marking their territory
          asserting their Freedom of the City
as one owner watches expressionless

I'll find Lizzie again in Australia
I leave her parents here

last stop

Margaret part-owns this popular guesthouse
where young men from Germany and France
return each year for her lavish breakfasts
                    and conversation

born in the South
            she has lived here all her life
thinks peace will still take thirty years
though some schools are integrated at last
            it used to be no houses, no jobs for us
            now it's different and they hate it

the Troubles are economic she tells me –
there are no murals or flags
                    in the leafy suburbs
where orange and green are neighbours –
will end now the South is wealthy
she'll probably go there soon
                    they care for their old folk

she checks I have sufficient blankets
            brings me pills when I catch cold
is due to leave on holidays
            the night before my plane goes
the place will be deserted
            I'll put your breakfast in the kitchen
            shut the door when you go

the land of gold

leaving

A rare opportunity is here presented for the emigration of
respectable single females to Victoria. . . . as successful diggers
usually get married as fast as circumstances permit, the few women
who arrive are usually soon removed from servitude
                              Armagh Guardian, Nov, Dec 1852

leaving was in the air:
after the famine half Ireland sailed away

with her brothers in the army
her father recently dead a sickly sister and brother
                    Lizzie must find work
how could a lively girl resist gold-rich Victoria?

my mother told me Lizzie sailed for New Zealand
                    to visit a married sister
met a man on board and left with him at Geelong

my cousin learnt that Lizzie
                    planned to come with friends
who changed their minds but still she came

the facts are simpler:
                    she set off alone arrived alone

where once our respectable family couldn't countenance
a seventeen year old girl sailing alone to be a servant
we exult in it

arrival

after fourteen weeks
            cramped between decks
the Roaring Forties gales
the wintry pounding of Bass Strait
the turbulent passage
                    through the Rip –

the reflective waters of the bay
the calm of gentle slopes
               and treeless shore
to the north she sees those pyramid hills
the markers of this large and tranquil space
              the You Yangs

when the anchor drops beside
the sandy spit Maloppio (*men going fishing*)
               now called Point Henry
she looks across Corio Bay
         to the vibrant town beckoning
the hundred servant girls on board

this first view of her new home
                holds no terrors
she decides for happiness

women going fishing

the promised husbands
               were not at Point Henry
not on the lighters taking them
                    across the bay
not at the Yarra Street pier
                nor on the wagons
carrying them uphill to the depot
or if they were
            the young girls didn't know

first they must pay for their passage
               in floors scrubbed
meals cooked cows milked
              and babies soothed
domiciliary servants to their sponsors
                sometimes more

Lizzie was optimistic – and fortunate
Charlie Wyatt her employer
a well-liked man with a new wife
on a farm four miles from Geelong
rations and twenty-one pounds
             for six months' work

two months after she was free
            the husband appeared
she stopped him in the street to ask directions
twenty years older but admitting to ten
a Londoner who made top hats
             and went to her church
that was enough

the garden of Geelong

one of the most
beautiful valleys in the world

> *Captain Foster Fyans*

once the hills of Anakie erupted molten rivers
                to cover the land with riches
then streams of liquid gold added their wealth:
Moorabool that *ghost river where the curlews call*
              Barwon *the magpie* or
the great stream running from mountains to sea
          a place for the dangerous Mindie to rest

below the steep hill Booneewang,
         where Moorabool and Barwon meet
the Wathaurongs gathered for ceremonies
before the rich soil became Geelong's garden
and they were exiled or destroyed

                  grapes and cherries were planted
violets and carnations
            wallflowers and camellias
an apple tree grafted with 120 varieties
          and the land became Fyansford

into this *Eden*
        the girl from Portadown came
to a settlement of three pubs
               an Anglican church
and Frogmore Farm with its
        kookaburra curlew and parrot
goanna and kangaroo
        a spring of yellow blossom
an autumn with scarcely a fallen leaf

on the Barabool Hills across the Barwon
Mr Robert Morrice released seven skylarks

Frogmore

a Melbourne man now owns the Wyatt place
where Lizzie lived and worked in 1853
yes go up
the owner's there
the long drive is lined with sugar gums

parking my Laser near the smaller gate
I see a bluestone mansion
                        set in a garden of giant trees
make my way across a lawn miles wide
to a group watching from the verandah
I explain I'm searching for my grandmother

of course, I'll show you round –
Heine the German poet was an ancestor –
but first a drink? a cup of tea?

in the old rooms facing the river
               Lizzie scrubbed these floors I walk on
at eighteen she was full of energy
                      accustomed to hard work
surprised to have good food
I hope her mistress Mary Ann was kind

everyone spoke well of Charlie
               no one mentioned his wife
until a spring wagon fatally capsized
on Fyansford Hill and she was noticed

Lizzie left before the house gained
        the bluestone wing
and gardens and nursery became famous.
when Charlie imported
                phylloxera-carrying vines
and the State's vineyards were destroyed
        Frogmore was suddenly infamous

the new owner plans to restore the basalt terraces
        now thick with thorns and periwinkle
has failed to save an old majestic pine
but other ancient trees
                saplings in Lizzie's time
surround the house –
laurel Chinese elm oak a mighty Araucaria
and my search has kept Lizzie alive

Christ Church Geelong

The oldest Anglican Church in Victoria on its
original site

she was devoted to the Church of Ireland
        and this was the next-best thing
though only six years old
            with no lichen or patches of moss
it was already too small for an expanding town

certainly not as grand as St Marks looming
        above their cottage in Portadown
but it was solid stone with a tower

a year and three days after she sailed
        her goal was accomplished –
she married John Freeman here in 1854

on a sunny winter's day
            I sit in the same cedar pews
now darkened and polished
         by years of worshippers
today's coloured windows were then clear glass
today's nave was their church
I stand where they stood at the altar

I'm sure he wore a smart top hat he'd made
she the dress of finest Irish linen she'd brought
tomorrow they would leave for the goldfields

myths

do top hats make you rich?

a family story says John poured
a hatful of sovereigns into
his wife's lap on their wedding day

Geelong was a boom town where
the wealthy wanted signs of their success
did that include top hats?

why then would those newlyweds
smiling on the Christ Church steps
leave so soon for Ballarat?

was it gold fever?
or were the sovereigns few –
can one or two pour down?

or is this another fiction
like Lizzie sailing for New Zealand
meeting John on board the boat?

my cousin and I review the stories –
John was not aboard the Mooltan
there was no New Zealand sister

we must abandon
the shipboard romance
decide to keep the sovereigns flowing

gold fever

the ancients warned us:

stiffen with gold
a rose a songbird a daughter
and know the agony of Midas!
mansions in Majorca
facility at polo
will not redress the cost

Jason could only steal the golden fleece
because a musician calmed the dragon
and a woman used herbs to make it sleep

we learn too late the price of our collusion

in what river must we bathe
                              to undo our Midas-wish?
not the once rich Yarrowee
              which led sober men to frenzy
or Dog Trap Creek which kept
                            a quiet Londoner
chasing his nugget for over twenty years
or today's south bank of the Yarra
              where hopefuls from everywhere
take the Casino's one chance in a million
to leap beyond the mean

perhaps only Lethe or Styx will cure it
or we could visit Mimir's well to remember
how gold is absent from our moments of bliss

driving to Ballarat

if I hadn't double booked the night before
if I hadn't felt guilty at missing a friend's Launch
if I hadn't searched frantically for a lost library book
if I hadn't stayed awake all night planning my trip
if I hadn't left sleepy-eyed in the morning dark
if I hadn't encountered thick fog and torrents of rain
if I hadn't kept driving to have coffee at Nhill
I mightn't have nodded off at the wheel
three hundred yards from my planned roadside stop

if I hadn't been in the town's 60km zone
if I hadn't been in a solid low Toyota
if the highway hadn't been clear of cars and trucks
if I'd been deaf and unable to hear the sound
of tyres on the broken edge of the tarmac
or too deeply asleep to feel the change
I mightn't have managed to avoid the post
wrestle the car back onto the road
drive the few yards to the Caltex station
fill up with petrol order coffee
and begin to read a two weeks old Herald Sun

next morning dull cold and wet
the loveliest dawn I've seen

no remote

even the pine tree bends before
this Ballarat rain

my cabin is waterproof
but I complain about everything else:
the heater doesn't work
hot water takes five minutes to come
the fridge starts with earthquake tremors
before settling to a freight train roar
the TV has no remote
the phone across a flooded courtyard
       takes coins when I have cards

I'm here because of Lizzie who in 1854
       had only a tent against the rain
freezing in winter scorching in summer
an open fire for cooking
no icebox in summer
            no Coolgardie yet
dipping water from a polluted stream
       or buying it by the bucket
to carry on muddy or dusty tracks
sometimes on slippery boards
          around deep holes
worst of all a husband with gold fever

Ballarat

nothing prepared her
for the scrubby rises and gullies
the dull tents climbing the sides of hills
the strange cylindrical sails bringing air
                    to ever deepening shafts

the sound of picks and cradles
                            horses and dogs
iron buckets and axes shouts and thuds
                    fights and songs
the Sabbath was quieter when work was banned
though sly grog brought its own commotion

Lizzie was used to mud
but not the mud of these crab-holed
                            flats and rises
these dun-coloured mounds around black pits
            where treasure drowned in water

that Ballarat rain – spear-points driven by the wind
                    a steadily falling screen
or drizzling creeping with cold into the tent

summer was dust mosquitoes
                    flies and polluted water
the sun inducing craziness

                    stubbornly they stayed
their first child born in the flimsy tent
heir they hoped to a fabulous fortune

Eureka

when they arrived
the diggers were in dangerous mood
        for heavy licences
taxed the searcher not the finder
and the easy gold had gone

Bendigo had already rioted
        now at Ballarat
ten thousand miners at one meeting
two thirds of the field

time to burn the licences
and take an oath:
We swear by the Southern Cross
to stand truly by each other
and fight to defend our rights and our liberties

a massive licence hunt next day
rage over a digger shot
and three innocent men in gaol
soldiers breaking the Sabbath the miners kept –
and men died under their new flag

John must have been at the meeting
the family story is clear:
though he planned to go to the stockade
        he was not at Eureka –
his young wife hid his trousers

easy to sympathise with her
                so far from home
married a mere eight months
she didn't need to be a martyr's widow
                but could there be another reason?

did this daughter of Ulster protestants
take the Government side
                against the miners' Irish leaders?

all we know is that John stayed home

the flag

the miners fought under
a white lawn Southern Cross
on finest blue woollen mohair
first flag of their own

not a polished production nor elegant
but the three women who made it
two Anastasias and one Anne
used the best materials in Ballarat

it flew over their rough stockade
one December Sunday
as one hundred and twenty men
and some families lay sleeping
expecting to be safe on the Sabbath

it flew over the soldiers
as they bayoneted wounded men
not once but scores of times
shot innocent bystanders outside the palisade

though holes appeared in its stars
it flew until hauled down by Trooper King
to be carried almost forty years later
by striking shearers in Barcaldine

today it's the star of the Ballarat gallery
somewhat moth-eaten after a curator
cut out bits of the blue for souvenirs

Lizzie's bullet

yes family stories agree –
a bullet went through Lizzie's
high bonnet as she stepped
                    outside the tent

violence was everywhere
diggers fought diggers
over claims
            over theft
                    over women

diggers fought Joes
over licenses
            over bullying
                    over rules

women fought women
over men
            over goods
                    over honour

men and women fought
across their time-honoured gulfs

a society where men fired off their guns
each evening for maintenance and warning

I don't know if Lizzie's bullet
came from a random fierce dispute
            or a routine cleaning gone wrong
its story continues to grow

treasure

the polished wooden box
so carefully lined
                with silk
could harbour fine jewellery
a baby's portrait
            delicate china
                    a trophy

John Freeman's pistol lies inside
his only legacy
handed down to his son William
and his son John
            and his son Wilfred

was this the gun
he planned to carry at Eureka?
was it this so carelessly discharged
            at the daily cleaning
that sent the bullet
            through Lizzie's headgear?

the family would never allow such a story
remember only the bullet and bonnet
                    treasure the gun

education at Sovereign Hill

gold can be beaten to 1/282,000th of an inch and one ounce
    of gold
can be drawn into eighty kilometres of wire

the Welcome Stranger is the biggest nugget in the world
Ballarat's Bakery Hill nugget the second

gold dust is the name of two low-growing garden plants
and *the gold of pleasure* is a European weed

the Golden Number is the method used to fix Easter
and the Golden Legend is a collection of saints' lives

there is a Lucky Woman's creek near Linton where fortunes
    were made
but unlucky nurses at Kalgoorlie had only two pints of
    water a day

Sun Loong in Bendigo is the world's longest ceremonial
    dragon
and St George with his dragon was on UK sovereigns
    from 1816

Clunes is circled by twenty-two extinct volcanoes and
    candles must be
dipped twenty times in paraffin at seventy degrees

Buninyong

was a town when Ballarat was a sea of mud
a timber town and way station
to places further west and north

John and Lizzie were among
thousands who followed the gold
to the Union Jack and Green Hill leads

above them the old volcano stretched:
Bonang Yowang to the Kulin
the man lying with his knees up

no warrior guardian this
but a casual watcher over
the desperate mêlée on the plain below

Thrice Blest
the town could celebrate in story
its soil springs and gold

the gardens at its centre boast
here rich and poor together meet
the cemetery has a better claim

Whim Holes

nothing whimsical about the hunt for gold
      with few surface nuggets to be found
hard work for the first diggers of 1858
those Canadians who brought
horse-drawn cylinders called whims
      to lift earth and the frustrating water
from underground gold-bearing streams

yet some fancy took a Londoner his Irish wife
      and their two *native sons*
south from the ordered town of Buninyong
to a series of holes in the ground
      in the middle of dense forest

they settled on a small block
not far from today's Little Hard Hills pub
      which shuts on a Monday
as I discovered by chance after a long wait –
they don't believe in notices

the Canadians left soon after they came
      with or without their whims
and some barbarian changed
      the settlement name to Enfield
but the far-from-fanciful Freemans
      stayed for thirty years

immigrants

rabbits and thistles we did not need
curses on the men who brought them!

skylarks are different:
on their release in 1854
the Argus gave a prize for the first hearing –
an Antipodean cuckoo in spring

after the wattlebirds' harsh rattle
the screech of rainbow lorikeets
the ravens' unbearable dying fall
even the musical chortle of magpies
immigrants waited for its ethereal voice

the Irish woman walks the muddy track
through forest to the goldfields store
she hears far above the pulse of heaven
a sustained clear song of runs and trills –
cornfields orchards Armagh

settled

if gold fever took them from a settled job in Geelong
                    to the wildness of the diggings
if the fever helped them follow the rush to Ballarat
                    Buninyong and then Whim Holes

it didn't last for long
               perhaps the children anchored them
perhaps the dream of riches faded
small house and garden security enough

sometimes John was a miner
sometimes a splitter in the timber trade
sometimes a labourer
sometimes an invalid

Lizzie's unchanged work was constant
               with skills learnt on the diggings
to keep a family fed and clothed
              to help at illness birth and death

mother to ten healthy children
yet signatures on a school petition
               and a few birth certificates
are her only marks on Whim Holes' history

the teacher

how to educate their children?
Lizzie and John signed petitions for a school
set in a small clearing in the forest
the tiny shack no bigger than a living room
Whim Holes Common School 1863
was for all denominations
unusual in those sectarian days

their youngest daughter Sarah
                an intelligent helpful child
loved school and received at eleven
her Certificate of a Child Sufficiently Educated
soon was a monitor teaching the beginners
                in the sun-drenched schoolyard

after her Sixth Grade the master suggested
she become a teacher
                too hot she said

scrubbed floors and washed dishes for a squatter
until saved by the Salvation Army
she taught other lessons
                                faced a different heat

illness

the widowhood avoided at Eureka
came near again in 1881
            when John was very ill

this time Lizzie was a matron of forty-six
               with ten children
to help manage their small farm
and the older boys could earn those extras
            Fijians call *the relish*

John worked again but four years later
they were in Ballarat for another four years
of Lizzie's nursing skills

most diggers had short lives
           with *miner's phthisis* common
John lasted here thirty six years
          before his death from typhoid

he was supposed to have wealth enough
to support his family through the invalid years
owning land in Ballarat and Melbourne's CBD
but there's no evidence –
the Enfield house was valued at six pounds
their rates five shillings

Lizzie was John's treasure

Blood & Fire

They have stormed our sinful cities ...

Henry Lawson: *Booth's Drum*

enthusiasm – possession by a god –
was breaking out all over
crackling down the streets like
the fire of the Salvation Army motto
spilling down the lanes

it could be the Orange Order marches
again – the bands drums hymns
the banners even the uniforms
Irish youths in Sydney presumed the links
as they attacked the Salvation standard-bearer
for orange in the colours

but this Army was at war with Satan:
fighting to rescue the poor in the gutter
people beyond the churches' reach
feeding bodies as well as souls –
anyone who hasn't eaten today, come to my home

the Corps marched from their Citadels after *knee drill* –
the Death & Glory Boys Daniel's Band
The Invincibles The Victors The Joshuas
The Conquering Host The Redeemed Warriors
The Royal Blood Washed
firing their volleys at the enemy
forty Devil's agents captured in Hobart

undeterred by Satan's weapons of soot
flour rotten eggs and fruit
heedless of black eyes broken noses and jaws
the sisters have to share the blows with the brothers

from the War Cry June 16 1883:
Thirty soldiers gave the message among stones, glass bottles,
mud, kerosene tins and rubbish . . .
roughs smashed into the ring, knocked and pushed,
threw clouts then six dead fowls.
We sang for Jesus for speaking was impossible.
A dead dog exploded. I stood
with one foot on each side of the dog and sang Beulah Land.

the Freeman children were early soldiers
in the King's Own Ballarat Corps
the Standard has been raised
recruits are pouring in

the true religion

when her sons and then her daughter
       with no ties to that other land
leapt into the zealous
       new Salvation Army
she was appalled
prayed each night for their return
          to *the true religion*
where the liturgy linked her with home

when she saw her children's lively faith
the heady zest of these new warriors –
one thousand mourners marched
her young son Thomas to his grave
with a song composed in his honour

when at the next service she presented
coins from his pockets as an offering
she knew she too must be a soldier

the new order

The Mayor has put his foot, so to speak, through
the drums ... of the Salvation Army.

The Argus 1891

hard to recall Matins in St Marks
where she sat in the same church
as the gentry (though further back)
such a decorous religion

Portadown was overthrown
as she followed her children
        into this rowdy new Army
where soldiers marched
without the Mayor's permission
went willingly to gaol protesting
their right to do the Lord's work

whatever town support was with the Mayor –
and the drums made a horrible noise
causing chaos among the horses –
it melted when the leaders were gaoled
especially attractive eighteen-years-old
        Lieutenant Eva

Lizzie's previous Bishop
        brokered a compromise
but never again would she worship
        with the City Fathers

I doubt that Lizzie marched or went to gaol
but the wild excitement of conflict
with taunts and missiles
drums and bands louder than ever
          exposed the unbridgeable gulf
from the sombre worship at home

her heart must stay with her body
learn this new way to worship God

the convert

once she made the change it was complete
a soldier now in God's Army
she accepted all the military discipline:
officers must obtain permission for courting
must only marry officers
women will take their husband's rank

after the death of her officer son's wife
he fell for an Army *lassie*
a fine woman a dedicated recruit but
                                        not an officer

like royalty Captain Edwin must choose
                                        between love and work
and like a later king
                                        he chose love and resigned
Lizzie was furious
as converts become more Catholic than the Pope

she didn't speak to Edwin for some time
until her heart defeated that intolerance
                                        learnt back home

Captain Sarah

Godly women possessing the necessary gifts and
qualifications ... shall be eligible for any office
and to speak and vote at all official meetings.
                                    Salvation Army rules

it didn't happen
they succeeded better than other churches
                    even managed a general
but they couldn't move too far ahead of their times

they offered a new world
            to bright young working girls
until marriage defeated them
            though they would have said
defeat is impossible for the Lord's army

take Lizzie's daughter Sarah
at twenty she trained to be an officer
            was chosen for the Flying Squad
which made special *raids* to help country Corps
within three months a Captain
                    in charge at Gundagai
soon she was leading the work in Temora
a mining town of twenty thousand souls to save

she knew the firepower of tomatoes and rotten fruit
            rotten's alright it's the good that hurts
the tiny salary which seldom came
the constant orders from Headquarters
to collect more money sell more papers
                    save more souls

on the back of a photo of two
        uniformed women arm in arm
she has written *Captains Freeman and Johnson
        both for hard* goes

at her marriage to Captain David
they took as their motto *God First*
never retracted that vow

David was second to God
she the assistant who bore nine children
yet ran the women's work and the corps
        when he was sick or away

a calm foil for her anxious husband
she could laugh at life's oddities
always *happy for storms*
ready to *fire a volley*

no longer Captain Sarah
        she died Mrs Major Southwell

Public Records Office

wipe your feet before you enter
no food no drink no pens
this is a temple where dry bones live

we lift their cardboard coffins from the shelves
open with reverence the *serried ranks*
where Lizzie's daughter Bella Campbell
lies between Brunt and Carney

thin Thomas Freeman
Lizzie's youthful son is squashed
between fat Fraser and a chubby Grout

among the dreary pale blue forms
on half a page torn from a notebook
Nurse Wheeler's competent hand
transcribes his almost final words

he leaves his mother all his small estate
his signature the day he died is firm and dark
hers trembles and scrawls across and down
the page her name unreadable
the last syllable *man* is barely there
her husband died three weeks ago

she gives the hospital a tenth of Tom's estate
which it records with thanks

I make a copy of these fading forms
                    trying to steady my hand

to my beloved ...

to learn of people
study their wills

Lizzie's careful daughter Isobel
itemised her legacy:

to my daughter Lilian
I give my sewing machine watch bedroom furniture

to my daughter Elizabeth
I give my brooch clock and family picture

to my daughter Florrie
I give my chinaware and cutlery

to my said daughters I give in equal shares
all my bed and table linen

Lizzie's husband John had many
years of illness yet died without a will

young Thomas dictating his in hospital
left his mother all he owned

and Lizzie? often daughters were left money
while sons received the bulk of the estate

she bequeathed each son a little cash
her daughters almost all her property

she had few treasures to disperse
each daughter gained a piece of Irish linen

and Captain Sarah the youngest living child
received her grandmother's Irish letters

lullaby

what do you carry from Ireland
when you leave at seventeen?
Lizzie brought
fine linen for her wedding dress
and her mother's lullaby

bye o bye o dear little baby

she sang it to Sarah and the others
first in a Ballarat tent then
in the house in the Whim Holes forest

Sarah sang it to my mother
who sang it to me
when the fierce Truby King decreed
we should lie screaming in our cradles
until time for our four-hourly feeds

she is such a darling baby

I walked the midnight floor
crooning it to my children
to the rustle of tropic palms
later sang it to my grandchildren
at an easier hour in a cooler place

will they remember?

the pelican

after you see the first they're everywhere
mostly in War Memorials sometimes in churches

in plaster stone and brass a pelican with head to breast
pecking – in times of scarcity – her blood to feed her chicks

I pass them almost daily by the War Memorial
surrounded by pansies or petunias in season

the image puzzles me: those soldiers we honour
were not mothers feeding their young

or is Christ the Pelican – see page 72 of *Symbols* –
his self-sacrifice offering us manna in heaven?

what of the pelican in Ballarat New Cemetery (1867)

not many carried past in plumed carriages
made sacrificial deaths – avoided them if possible

or is Christ a mother gathering her chicks?
I'd prefer a mother to a shepherd greeting me

ornithologists say that pelicans never peck blood from
        their breasts

as you sow

Lizzie
for twelve years –
more than four thousand days –

your mother had no letter
uncertain if the ship went down
or where or how you were

were you too poor to write
(where now those golden guineas?)
or did your letters go astray?

she hadn't changed address
did it hurt to think of home?
were you angry when you left?

although so poor
she wrote five times
did you receive her letters?

after your mother thought you dead
she replied the day your letter came
without reproach

your brother was not so kind
writing from India:
You must have been in a frightful out of the way place
when you could not manage to send a letter in ten years
for in the wildest parts of this country
there is means of Communication

but as you sow etc

George your youngest child
heir to his father's dangerous fever
headed for Coolgardie's Rush

he never wrote
is buried somewhere West
you died without knowing

a winter's morn at Lake Wendouree 1901
after the painting by George Reynolds (1854–1939)

an old woman in white apron and red shawl
carries an armful of twigs round
the lake made from a swamp
                and a drowned creek

Lizzie could be gathering sticks for her fire –
different from the peat fires of Armagh
but the flare of her twigs will set
                the bigger logs ablaze

she knows the satisfaction of small gains
small intimacies and ecstasies –
                something for nothing

how they get the faces they deserve
after the painting of that title by John Brack

if she were a horse
my father would buy her –
those big green-blue eyes are wide apart

so often said to be sparkling as in Irish
they are steadier in this photo of old age
after years of clearly looking at the world

my mother and grandmother have eyes
like hers – I missed out
but see them in my daughter

neat ears set flat against her head
wide nostrils straight nose
bulbous at the end – her gift to me?

her mouth is a generous bow
at once smiling and sad
as in *mavourneen mavourneen*

her unlined face is framed by wavy hair
escaping a high bonnet
with bands twined in an almost Celtic knot

over a plain bodice the intricate
pattern of lace
is held by a brooch at her neck

can it be gold? a trophy perhaps
of the long mining years
or bought with the mythical sovereigns?

a good midwife a mother her children loved
rescuer at a fatal accident
she worked hard to acquire this face

Got to pul in my Hornes

the photograph catches her
                    standing on her veranda –
ankle length skirt over a darker blouse
the same fussy buttons and bows
                    as in other photos
the same high bonnet with its Celtic straps

hands clasped at her tiny waist
head just a little forward on sloping shoulders
                    her gaze artless and direct
she seems content with her simple cottage
the flowers in its unkempt garden
a block of wood holding the window open
and the side gate tied up with wire

she's no warrior

she lives alone
a letter says *no company for Easter*
sons visit granddaughters too though some
would come more often if I had money

                    she misses her daughters
though poor she sends a postal note
                    to Captain Sarah
Sarah though poor sends it back
so Lizzie sends another

she can't help her daughter at Mt Rowan
i am not able for milk work now
i have got an old woman on me
Got to pul in my Hornes
i have not been to the army for 2 weeks
        but i am well in my soul
thanks be to God
        that we can have Christ at home

and all the trumpets

*One of our oldest warriors, Sister Freeman has
been promoted to glory.*
  Ballarat North Salvation Army Corps newsletter

in this army you don't die
                    you're promoted
if you are an officer
you have already been promoted
            to Captain or Colonel
or the top job of General

as a soldier on the bottom rung
Lizzie has the biggest leap to heaven
although two officer children may
                have won for her a notch or two

relatives wear white at her funeral
                    since it is a celebration
the band plays Beulah Land
for they know she will wake in glory

her bones lie with her husband and son
on a rise in the New Cemetery
with a wide view
            to her daughter's Mt Rowan farm
Tandragee is far away

below her the solid respectable city
which she knew as mud and chaos
to the south Mt Buninyong
                    below whose shelter
she camped in the early days
to the east Warrenheip twin sentinel

under these volcanoes she fought for God
until it was time to go Home

Chronology

Elizabeth Grimason
born August 12th 1835 at Tandragee, County Armagh
one of seven children of
Thomas a carpenter and weaver and Elizabeth Holmes a spinner
the family soon moved to Portadown

she sailed on the Mooltan for Geelong from Southampton 23 April 1853
arrived Point Henry 3 August 1853
domestic servant to Charles Wyatt of Frogmore, Fyansford
for six months
married John Freeman at Christ Church Geelong on 26 April 1854

they left soon after for Ballarat goldfield
first child Jack was born in a tent 12 December 1855
moved to Buninyong where William
their second child was born 26 Sept 1857
moved to Whim Holes 1858–9
twin daughters born 11 October 1859
between 1862 and 1874 six more children born

they left Whim Holes, now Enfield, for Ballarat 1886
John aged 74 died from typhoid fever 21 April 1890
son Thomas aged 28 died of typhoid fever 15 May 1890
daughter Isabella aged 41 died 28 August 1905
Elizabeth lived at Creswick Road next to the Royal Oak Hotel 1906
Elizabeth aged 74 died 5 February 1910
is buried with John and Thomas
in Ballarat's New Cemetery

Acknowledgements

The epigaph is from Gustaf Sobin's essay 'Basso Continuo' in *Heat* 1 New Series, 2001. I am indebted to Judith Wright's poem 'Eli Eli' (*Collected Poems 1942–1970*) for the last two lines on page 7. 'art & life' was published in *Hecate* and 'the colonisers' in *LiNQ*.

My thanks are due to my cousin, Margaret Pickard, for her small monograph on Elizabeth Grimason and for making available Elizabeth's and her mother's letters. I am grateful for two grants from Arts SA, which enabled me to visit the relevant places of Elizabeth's life and to seek help from other relatives and countless librarians and Records Office staff in Northern Ireland, London and Victoria. My thanks too to Varuna and Booranga Writers' Centres for Fellowships which provided perfect environments for writing.

So many friends and family here and in London have generously assisted this project with information, critical comment and space for writing. Susan Hampton has been a most helpful editor. Finally, my heartfelt thanks to my writing group and especially Ruth Raintree. Their support never wavered during my long involvement with Lizzie.